JAMES VS DAREK

BY

JAMES GREEN

James vs. Darek

James vs. Darek/James Green

ISBN-13: 978-0615794181

ISBN-10: 061579481

DDA PUBLISHING

www.ddapublishing.com

James vs. Darek

TABLE OF CONTENTS

INTRODUCTION 5

MY PRAYER 6

ME (PART ONE) 8

BROTHERS (PART ONE) 11

LARD 14

APART 16

PERFECT 17

A MEMORY 20

HEARTBREAK 23

ME (PART TWO) 25

BROTHERS (PART TWO) 29

3 31

MY ADDICTION 33

THE SWITCH 36

TROIS 39

TENSION 41

TORN 43

CHEATER 46

DEAR WOMEN 48

DILLAN 52

GRANDMA 56

JAMES VS DAREK 58

THE COUNTDOWN 62

THE SECRET 65

BODY ART 71

FOR YOUR THOUGHTS:

THE CLUB 74

THE SOCIAL NETWORK 76

MIRROR 80

30 81

THE CLINIC 82

PERCEPTION 85

GOOD 87

MATRIMONY 88

MMXIII 91

CHOICE 94

TIME 97

BIGGEST FEAR 99

BONUS MATERIAL

YOU 101

"SHE" 104

INTRODUCTION

Welcome to my world. What you are about to encounter are simply my thoughts. These thoughts have been harboring inside of me for many, many years now. Some of them are good, some are…not so good. I've never really had the opportunity to share them with anyone until now. I never thought anyone would take the time to listen or attempt to understand. I don't know if this would be considered poetry, or they are just simply my thoughts that happen to rhyme. Either way…they are me.

James Green

MY PRAYER

Dear God,

Remember me?

I know I'm your biggest disappointment...

Can you send your son to set me free?

I was going to say my normal prayer

But I needed to apologize

For all the wrong that I've done

For the cheating, the stealing, and the lies

I've taken this body you gave me

I made it fat and scared it with tattoos

Sometimes I wish there wasn't free will

That way I didn't have the power to choose

I hope there's room for me in heaven

If not...I'll understand

That my addictions were the thing that
held me back

And that I failed you...

As a man

Amen

ME (PART ONE)

What you're looking at

What you see

This is what I believe is me

I'm shy and I'm soft

And afraid of the world

I wouldn't know the first thing to say to
a girl

Some say I'm spoiled

But I just learned how to get my way

I enjoy drawing and cartoons

And going outside to play

I'm alone most of the time

And that creates problems

When no one is around

Who is supposed to solve them?

I talk to myself

And usually answer myself back

But who is that talking

When my room is all black

I was picked on and teased

About my weight and my hair

I would go home and cry

And that voice would be there...

BROTHERS (PART ONE)

I've had the same friends

Since I was a kid

They were all closer than family

I remember all the things that we did

I appreciate my friends

But I'm feeling kinda blue

All my brothers are a phone call away

But I realized I'm missing two…

They said we looked alike

You were a little taller

The females liked you better

We both played on the regular, but you
were the much better baller

Your feet were a little bigger

Yet sometimes we swapped shoes

I remember we had some alcohol and safety
pins

And gave each other tattoos

When you started selling weed
I wanted to too
You sold me some seasoning
Yet I still forgave you

We stole things together
From radios to wheels
To cd's, to shoes
We paid for each other's meals

You installed my stolen radio
Then stole it back the same night
My people saw you from the window
And the truth came to light

I let it go and forgave you
Since I called you my brother
Your sister was like my sister
Your mother like my mother

I'm as loyal as they come

To anyone I call a friend

But it was time we finally parted ways

When you stole from me again

...But I still love you

LARD

To grow up fat

It is the worst pain on earth

How you look, how people treat you

Makes you want to reverse your birth

James vs. Darek

What's good tastes so bad

What's bad tastes so good?

I'd rather eat a cheese burger

Than some fiber bar that tastes like wood

I eat I eat I eat

And I don't know when to stop

I sit there after, watching TV

Feeling like I'm about to pop

No one knows a fat persons pain

They never hear our cries

I'm sitting here with a fork in my hand

And tears running down my eyes

APART

Apart of me is happy

Apart of me is not

Apart of me is the reason

I have everything I've got

Apart of me is evil

Apart of me is good

Apart of me does things I shouldn't

Yet encourages me that I should

I don't want that part of me anymore

Apart of me wants to kill it

But I'm willing to die before I let that
part of me take over

God will it

PERFECT

James vs. Darek

What's the perfect woman?

She's thick and knows how to cook

She passes up the club

For a bubble bath and a good book

What's the perfect woman?

I watch her walk and get a bulge in my pants

She's not intimidated by strippers

She already knows how to dance

What's the perfect woman?

She's classy and of course a freak

Even if you've been together for years

She f***s you at least 5 times a week

What's the perfect woman?

You cancel plans with your boys, because she's worth it

You get on one knee and give her that ring

Why?

Because she's perfect

A MEMORY

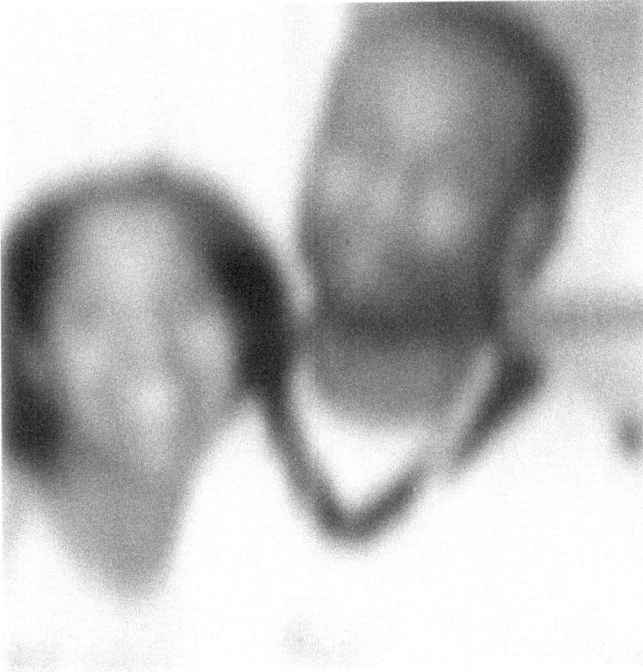

We made our vows in jeans

That should've told us it wasn't real

When I placed a ring on your finger

Wasn't it supposed to be a feeling I was
supposed to feel?

James vs. Darek

I told you I was in love with you
But I was in love with somebody else
I didn't want to see you with another man
So I kept you for myself

I knew she'd cheat on me while I was away
So I chose you instead
After all you were a good friend to me
And always kept me fed

There was a certain level of love
I knew we couldn't achieve
In the back of my mind I remember the day
I found out you slept with Steve

I planned another marriage
I was going to do it after we got a
divorce
My plan sounded so ignorant then
But back then I had no remorse

James vs. Darek

I cheated time after time

You finally left me

I admit you had some balls

You married him

And when it was time to marry my next wife

...she didn't answer my calls

HEARTBREAK

When my heart breaks I'm empty

It feels like I've just died

You'd only see my normal face

And never knew that I've cried

My love for you turns to hate

And that hate will pursue you

I'm protected, so it's out of my hands

What that hate will do to you

There's a monster in a cage

And it's deep inside of me

I'd attempt to keep it locked up

But I don't have the key...

ME (PART TWO)

What you see now is the suit I've created

It's built to endure pain

And the people I've hated

I don't age much

After all it's a suit

I highlight my attributes

And make sure that I'm "cute"

My eyes are innocent

And possess a certain skill

They can see deep into your soul

They can tell how you feel

The voice taught me some things

Like how to be tough

How to make money

How to conquer women

And other useless stuff

He gave me a style

Showed me how to use the law of attraction

How to get what I want

And give my flesh satisfaction

I don't work for anybody

I've been my own boss

But you see everything I've named

Has come with a cost

When I placed all my orders

I never looked at the price

I didn't know that in all this

I had to sacrifice my relationship with Christ

Now I want my life back

I don't know if I can reverse it

I don't know if God still loves me

I took what he gave me and perversed it

James vs. Darek

And now this is me

Alone, fighting this battle

I just want to go back to being that kid

Playing alone with his rattle

...God help me

BROTHERS (PART TWO)

Where do I begin?

I'm still pretty confused

That we parted over money

And both of us feel our "niceness" was abused

I can look you straight in the eye

And say I never stole a dime

You put in a lot of money towards my dream

I put in all of my time

We both took a risk

But I tried to take it all

I made a promise I couldn't keep

I can say I made a bad call

I tried to make your money back

I did everything that I could

I rushed on every move that I made

James vs. Darek

Knowing I shouldn't, but my heart said I should

I lost everything in my attempt

My cars, my stash, my house

Instead of talking face to face

I had to argue with your spouse

She called me a liar

And pretty much a thief

Insulted me to the core

I wanted to knock out her teeth

So now we are strangers

And we don't even speak

Our children don't even know each other...

...I'm sorry this hurts to bad, I can't finish this

But I still love you

3

How many you's are there

I know there's 3 of me

One of me is nice

One of them is E…

He doesn't like me to say the E word

Even though it's true

It's hard to look in the mirror sometimes

Knowing that isn't you

He came because of my pain

I've been hurt so many times

He came to protect me

Even if it meant committing crimes

If I liked a girl, I pointed

And just for me, he'd go and choose her

If she hurt my feelings or left me alone

He made sure she got pregnant by a loser

James vs. Darek

I know I can snap my fingers

And acquire a bunch of wealth

But is it worth any of it

When you are deathly afraid

...of yourself

MY ADDICTION

Ever since we first met

I've chased you everyday

I did what I had to do to get you

Nothing stood in my way

James vs. Darek

You've been like a drug to me

You've given me such a rush

Any words about leaving you

You cover my mouth

And say "hush"

We've been through it all

Whether there was someone else

Or just us

It's crazy after 25 years

I still have this little boy crush

It hurts to say I think we should break
up

Even though it makes me sad

But being with you isn't healthy

I saw what you did to my dad

You feel incredible and there's nothing
like you

But you've literally f***d up my life

You're the reason I have a child out of
wedlock

And the reason I lost my wife

I'm leaving now, I'm not coming back

For strength, I'm going to pray

She kicked the door closed, unfolded my hands

Knowing I wasn't strong enough yet…

"Ok, I'll stay"

THE SWITCH

My eyes roll back

I can feel him taking over

The Honda civic is now becoming a range rover

From the outside looking in

You'd probably never see

It would look like a second to you

But it feels like an eternity for me

My confidence is building

My spines becoming more erect

Voice is getting deeper

I can feel it taking effect

My heart rate is slowing down

Everything is moving slower

All though things are getting clearer

I can't wait til this is over

She raises her hand and orders a drink

The whole night I heard what she was saying

About how cheap her man is, so when her
drink came

I said "wait, I'm paying"

I slid the bartender a 50

I know she didn't know who I was

She asked me the occasion

I told her "just because"

The bartender brought my change back

But I already walked away

And had already slid my number in her
pocket

...I knew she'd call the next day

TROIS

Romance was gone

The sparks extinguished

Friendship was dying

Love itself was relinquished

His suitcase was packed

He was leaving after work

She was being as asshole

He was being a jerk

Her pride broke down

She sent him a text

He didn't respond

She knew what to do next

He headed home

Heart hurt and palms sweating

Replays of the arguments

Trying to concentrate on the forgetting

James vs. Darek

He opens the door

Knowing he's leaving the woman that once
was his world

And she was laying there naked

On his bed...with another girl

And he stayed

TENSION

James vs. Darek

They walk by each other not saying a word

When her back is turned, he gives her the bird

Tension builds on a daily basis

That's why he finds himself in different places

Temporary peace, then he goes back to his hell

He does it out of respect

Though he doesn't mean well

Everything she doesn't do

The next woman surely does

He buys other women things

Like flowers with a card that read "Just because"

He's smart, there's no proof

All evidence is deleted

But what would he do

If he found out that she had cheated...

TORN

James vs. Darek

One satisfies my physical

One satisfies my mental

One knows how to make my day

When the other one makes my day
detrimental

They both are beautiful

They both are fine

One knows about the other, the other one
doesn't

But as for now, they both are mine

They both get very jealous   :

And hate it when I'm away

But how do I please both of them

When there's only 24 hours in a day

One gives me stability

One is kind of a live wire

One gives me the feeling she'd do so

But ones been with me through the fire

James vs. Darek

One fulfills my fantasy

Keeping both would just be greed

But what am I to do?

Go with who I want...

Or who I need

CHEATER

We argue then I cheat

I'm one up yet feel defeat

I've got a story to tell my friends

But the moment is always bitter sweet

You complain I find another

We had sex, I met her mother

I had to let her go

Before you got the chance to discover

You trip and then I dip

She finds me I make her strip

You found a trace of her

But lies roll so easily off my lip

Here you go again

So I had sex with your friend

I fell in love with her

So we did it again and again

James vs. Darek

You asked to be my wife

But I already created a second life

Never thought I'd take my last breath

When you got a hold of that knife...

DEAR WOMEN

I'm sorry

I know I've misused you

I've used your bodies for myself

And mentally abused you

I've played the "good guy" role

Like I was better than others

I'd kill a man for doing what I've done to you

If he did it to my mother

I remember all your faces

The ones that I left scorn

But you must understand

My teachers have been society and porn

I mean we've had good times

We just did things all wrong

My justifications were I didn't hurt you

And hey, we get along

James vs. Darek

I only seem different

Because I know the works of the devil

I know the power of deception

So it just seems like I'm on another
level

You see all I have, and you assume that I
work hard

But all I ever did was ask

I learned how to play my cards

We didn't use a condom

And never got an infection

I leave you know worries, my love

You see I come with my own protection

I really do love all of you

And I really am sorry

I wanted it to be me and all of you

And maybe a red Ferrari

I hope you find the right guy

And he sweeps you off of your feet

You just have to forget about me, stop
being bitter

And be open to finally meet

Turn the TV off, open your bible

And then you'll clearly see

That the man you truly need

Is the total opposite of me...

DILLAN

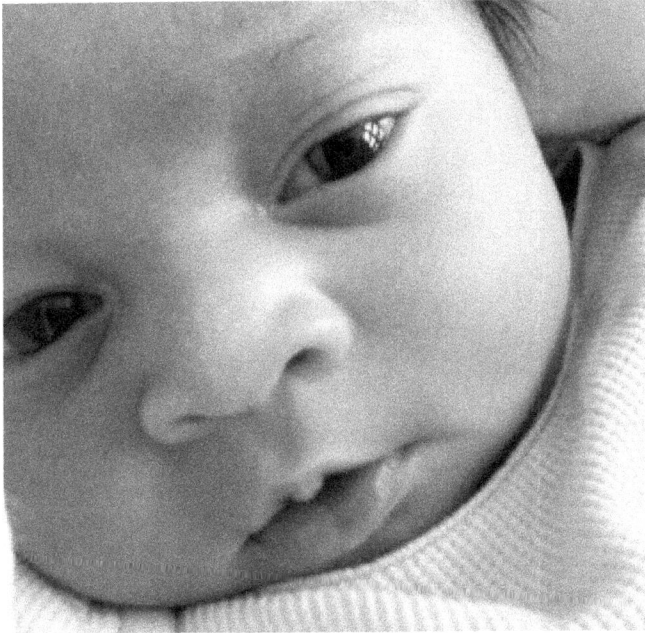

First thing I notice, are his big brown
eyes

Then I'm thrown off, by his annoying ass
cries

James vs. Darek

He turns and watches TV

Then I stare at his profile

I know every inch of his thoughts

Even though I've only known him for a
little while

There's a bothersome obsession

With keeping him safe

I pick his nose clean

I make sure his diaper isn't chafe

Every weekend

I give him chores

I can sleep like a baby

To the sound of his snores

His hair is like mine

His lips and his nose

There were ten million sperm

And he's the one that God chose

We had him the wrong way

James vs. Darek

We should've been married

Will we have to pay for it?

The thought of it is scary

I'll make sure he puts God first

And not make the mistake I that I did

Of ever having to wonder

If the story of Christ was a fib

Every Saturday we're on our knees

I tell him to pray

He says things like "thank you for the pizza"

When he hasn't even eaten for the day

I'll die before he fights the battles I fight

He'll never know what I've been through

I'll teach him to love everyone

Even if he doesn't know you

God showed me the light

And I'll give Dillan the key

It's just my biggest fear

That he'll turn out just like me

GRANDMA

When I got that call

Apart of me died

It didn't seem real that my grandma was
no longer alive

I was across the country

And couldn't say goodbye

My mom was being honest; I just wanted it
to be a lie

I dropped the phone

For a second I hated my mom

I know it wasn't her fault

But she dropped one hell of a bomb

Maybe it was her time

They had already taken her limbs

Her husband didn't seem too sad

Never knew what the deal with him

I miss her so much

It's making this hard to write

But if I don't get this out

I won't be able to sleep for the night

Wish you got to meet my son grandma

He looks and acts like me

I wish I could bring you back to meet him

But I know that could never be

I hope when it's time to go to heaven

I get to see you just once more

But the way I'm living my life grandma

Who knows what I have in store…

I miss you

JAMES VS DAREK

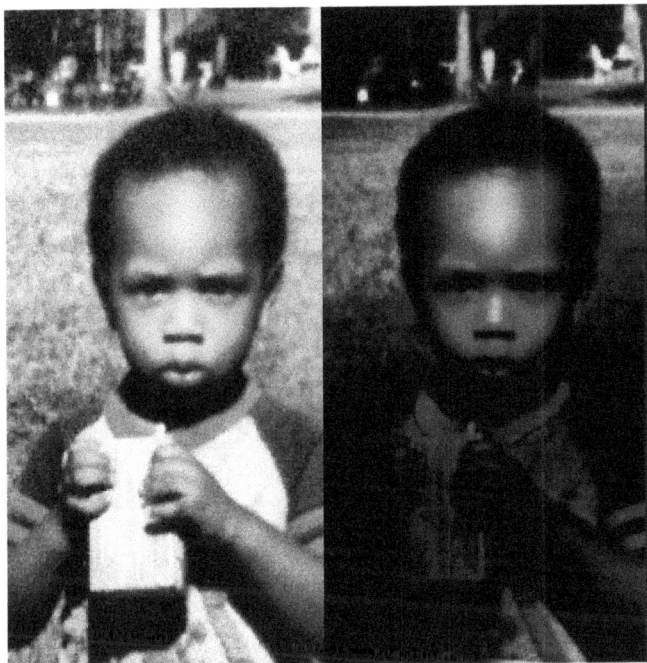

James vs. Darek

Darek is dying

Don't be sad

James is alive

With a piece of mind Darek never had

Darek wanted the world

And everything in it

James knows the world is just the world

And the sky is the limit

Darek's an honest hustler

But his mind stays on money

James is more relaxed

If you get to know him, he's actually
pretty funny

But don't get me wrong

James definitely has ends

But understands there are more important
things in life

Like family and friends

James vs. Darek

James has a dream of being like Martin
Luther King

Darek's cool with having a nice watch and
a ring

Darek is an addict

And sex is his drug

Be careful though, he can manipulate you

With something as simple as a hug

Every day Darek wakes up

And wonders who he will attract

He goes through his mental rolodex

And plans his attack

His method is simple

You may have heard of it, it's called
"The Secret"

But his secret shouldn't be a secret

And I can no longer keep it

If he knows who he wants

She will come by his will

He understands the power of the mind

James vs. Darek

It is by far his best skill

He misused the power of faith

And called it a different name

Since no consequences have happened yet

He considers it a game

But James was born

A soul needed to be saved

A change made in the world

It was time for Darek to behave

But Darek didn't want to

So now he has to die

Because when you hear James speak

Darek's actions make it seem like a lie

So don't be saddened by is death

Even if you miss Darek as a person

James is pretty much the same

Just a much better version

THE COUNTDOWN

James vs. Darek

One more sip

He thinks he can do it

No one will care anyway

Why not...screw it

No woman to call his own

No friends to converse with

No granddad

No grandmother that he could go to church
with

The barrel looks empty

But he knows what's down there

His finger is shaking

He doesn't want to be scared

So many tears

It's fogging up his vision

It's either him or everyone else

But he doesn't want to go to prison

James vs. Darek

Takes a last look at his mother's picture

And wipes his right eye

He takes a deep breath

His last words "bye-bye"

THE SECRET

James vs. Darek

Exposing myself is hard

But it's something I have to do

I hope you take what I say

As advice and a gift to you

You hear me say it a lot

A term called "The Law"

I used it for anything I wanted

Acquired things you've never saw

It's not a conspiracy theory

In actuality it's a scientific fact

If you think you can handle what I'm
going to tell you

Then relax, kick your feet up and sit
back

The smallest thing in the world

Are what you and I call atoms

This is a fact that we all know

That goes back to the beginning since
Adam

James vs. Darek

Those atoms are made up of protons and
electrons

And of course a nucleus

With a good enough microscope

You will see the truth to this

The electrons are floating around

And held to the nucleus by what

The term is called vibrations

I know what you're saying now...so what?

Everything on planet Earth

Is made up of vibrations

Only the combination of DNA changes

But everything has a relation

Now take the brain and take a cell phone

And watch how the two relate

They both send and receive signals at the
blink of an eye

No matter the city or state

James vs. Darek

The vibration of a phone goes in a
straight line

It goes from tower to phone

How the signal penetrates brick and
metal, scientists can't figure out

So let's leave that part alone

The brain signal is slightly the same

But instead of straight, it goes
everywhere, like a splatter

The signal is picked up by other brains

And actually affects physical matter

Now keep that in mind and take the law of
gravity

It is a physical law

What goes up must come down

You can give any example of anything you
saw

Now take for example an airplane

A bird or even a fly

They break the law of gravity with the
law of lift

James vs. Darek

You can see that with your actual eyes

There are laws that supersede others

The above facts should give you satisfaction

There is a law that supersedes every law

And that is the law of attraction

You receive what you send out

Just think of this little rhyme

It's a quote from Earl Nightingale

"You become what you think about most of the time"

So if you want a big house, think a big house

BELIEVE and it will come to you

The harder you think the faster it'll come

And before you know it, it's in front of you

Knowing these facts I misused the knowledge

And used it on women and things

James vs. Darek

It's easy to get caught up in this world

And not know the trouble it brings

I read about all the things Jesus did

And his abilities sounded the same

Then I realized the LOA was just a perverted version

And understood the Devil was the blame

Faith has limitless power

Before you try it, I beg of you pray

If you take the wrong path that I did, you'll regret it

Take heed to the words that I say

...I love you all

BODY ART

The first one I got was a dog

It meant absolutely nothing

It was my first time at a tattoo shop

I had to pick something

James vs. Darek

Next thing I got was a dragon

At the time it seemed pretty cool

But now I look at it and shake my head
and think

Damn, I must've been a fool

I have two passages from proverbs

Got those when my life got realistic

One of them regards the strength of faith

The other about being materialistic

My mother's name is on my wrist

By some guys I think were doing meth

The shop was so smelly that day

The whole time I had to hold my breath

John 3:16 is on my right shoulder

I want to finish it up with a sleeve

But it basically talks about the gift of
Jesus

And your award if you choose to believe

My favorite one is the face of my son

James vs. Darek

It's tatted on the left side of my chest

The bible's words mean the world to me

But for some reason it's more special
than the rest

My body is filled with different things

From messages, to portraits to fiction

Even though my messages mean well

I know it's a contradiction

God told me not to mark my body

I hope he knows I mean well

I hope my words save someone

Even if the cost

...is hell

FOR YOUR THOUGHTS:
THE CLUB

The lights are bright

And the stars are out

Everybody's wondering who's coming out

Drink after drink

Attempting to build courage

Alcohol plus rejection

Equals you not being discouraged

The bigger the ass, the higher the nose

More than likely the cheaper the house

The more expensive the clothes

They used to dance

Now they just take pics

And say they had a ball

When they stood there the whole time

And didn't do shit

James vs. Darek

The bartenders make out

The promoters break even

Facades are created; they're hoping
you'll believe in

High fives are given

Like you haven't seen them in years

But you saw them earlier that day

Always thought that was kinda weird

When the lights come on

The true faces will show

It's the time you find out

Who's really a ho

Then morning comes

You reminisce with your friends

6 days later

You do it all over again

THE SOCIAL NETWORK

My first social network

I made a page on Black Planet

It was so fun back then

But now I can't stand it

The poor claim to be rich

And the rich don't exist

And fighting evolved to tapping a
keyboard

Instead of an actual fist

All those classy women

They chose to become hos

They're souls are gone for "likes"

And gone are all their clothes

They yearn for attention

And a complementing comment

And then turn their noses up

And use the finger gesture, as if all
those "thirsty" men make her vomit

She "hates sleeping alone"

And her valentines date is her son

She takes pics of 350 dollars and maybe a
cute little pink gun

She makes model faces

And will never be in a magazine

In half of her a** naked pics

The room aint even clean

Haven't forgot about the men

Who "like" all of their pics

Who seemed to be born with no common
sense

And only think with their dicks

They say the same thing to you

That he said to her

But it's just a numbers game

It's all about who bites the bait first

Relationships last a week

Real love is fake

You see pics of TV dinners

From women who have no idea how to bake

A page full of text grams

And some of them are probably funny

But if you don't see any pics of themselves

They're probably fat or ugly

Bigger people take close up pics

And you can filter all of your flaws

You say things to people on there

That in person, you wouldn't have the balls

In all, its ok I guess

You can use it to promote

You can post positive things

You can encourage people to vote

But back in the day it was fun

James vs. Darek

And now it's not the same

It went from just connecting to old
friends

To one huge, terrible, no moral having

...sex game

MIRROR

Why do we judge?

When we are all the same

We'll all end up in the same place

And only have us to blame

Whether you're a gay or a thief

There's no difference between me and you

We've all sinned and deserve death

But there is one thing that is true

There was this guy that came

And took our death for us

And the only payback he asked for

What just for us to trust...

Why do we make that so hard?

30

For 30 years I thought

It was all about money and power

Women, jewelry and other things

Why does it feel so sour?

I buy what I want

I do what I want

But it feels like I don't have sh*t

Could it possibly be what I thought was life

Turned out not to be it?

What is it I'm missing?

I need an answer please

The first time I got an answer

They were unspoken words

It was when I bowed my head

...and fell on my knees

THE CLINIC

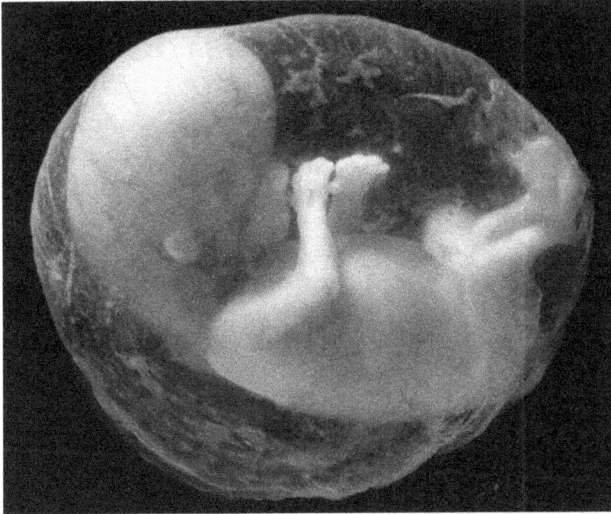

Sitting here in the dark

Not that long before I'm born

I'm anxious to see my mom

Maybe I'll see her in the morn

I wonder what I'll be

Maybe I'll be a big deal

I'll finally be rid of this tube stuck in
me

And be able to enjoy a real meal

I can't wait to meet my dad

Even though I've never heard his voice

I hope he isn't mad at me

I hope he knows it wasn't my choice

I hear my mommy crying

Something can't be right

She's usually sleep by now

She's crying and it's the middle of the
night

I guess I'm coming early

Let me turn around

I know I'm supposed to go head first

When I hear a particular sound

I'm waiting for the doctor to reach for
me

I'm looking for his hands

WAIT!!! WHAT IS THAT???

7 months of life

I guess I got my portion

If mommy loved me so much

Then why did she get an abortion?

PERCEPTION

Laying in a hospital bed

They had to remove my legs

I wanted the doctor to take my life

I begged and begged and begged

I'm lying here crying

Can't even get out of the bed

I look over and there's another guy
laying there

With a bandage around his head

Are you ok I asked him?

I'm in no pain but now I'm blind

I told him I hated the choice that I made

And how I wished I could press rewind

He tells me it's ok

He's proud of what he did

Are you crazy man, you'll never be able
to see your kid

I'll be ok he said

I can hear him and touch his skin

The most important thing to me

Is that I remain happy within

He's crazy

How can he be happy?

He's sitting there with no eyes

And then I hear the screams of children

They heard their father just died

And then I realized it could always be worse

Thank you lord

GOOD

Sex is good

Gay is good

Pork is good

Seafood is good

Orgies are good

Loving money is good

Porn is good

Alcohol is good

Weed is good

McDonalds is good

Our music is good

Our movies are good

I could go on and on…

And you'd say it's all about perception

I'd say the devil is no fool you fool…

That's the whole point of deception

MATRIMONY

There was a pattern laid out

We were all supposed to follow

We'd know if we picked up a book

And for once put down the bottle

We were to choose our mate early

Marry and make love

And have kid after kid

And it would always fit like a glove

We'd be together forever

The two of us would become one

And we'd live thousands of years

And have a limitless supply of fun

But in came the serpent

The one that created our fight

With a few subtle words

He made eve take that bite

James vs. Darek

So now we try to make right

In a world full of wrong

We barely get married anymore

Let alone get along

We see sex before we have it

We have it, then create a habit

And love floats away

So far we can't grab it

We watch TV and porn

Then pull out our checklist

If they aren't a thug or a stripper

It's a high chance you'll be dismissed

We take naked pics now

To give ourselves choices

There are no more real leaders

Entertainers are our voices

So we choose who we think

Is closest to what we saw

And we wonder why she slept with your best friend

Or why that man hauled off and broke your jaw

There was a plan for us

But we threw it in the trash

For a few "likes" on the net

And a strangers piece of a*s

So all these women sit there with all

These fatherless baby's in their carriage

Wondering why they never learned the point

And the true meaning of marriage

MMXIII

It's December 21

Dooms day is here

The city is full of chaos

Madness and fear

All the water is sold out

And the canned goods too

Tears fall from eyes

What are we going to do?

Some people turn to God

Some people turn to sin

There was somebody doing something

No matter what part of the city you were in

The countdown began

10, 9, 8

Some people were watching the news

Some were enjoying their last plate

7, 6, 5

Now it's getting real

People finally want to share with others

Exactly how they feel

4, 3, 2

Everyone braces

You can see the despair and hopelessness

On everyone's faces

1, 0!

They're waiting for something

An explosion, a fire

But there was absolutely nothing

Seems the Mayans were wrong

Could the bible be true?

That no one knows when that time is coming

And that there are some things that we should do

Nah, it can't be right, we need better
answers

Like whens the world going to really end '

Maybe find a cure for cancer

Let's ask this rich guy when the worlds
going to end

He looks up at the sky

He squints his eyes, folds his hands and
says

12-12-MMXIII

Good enough, let's believe him!

CHOICE

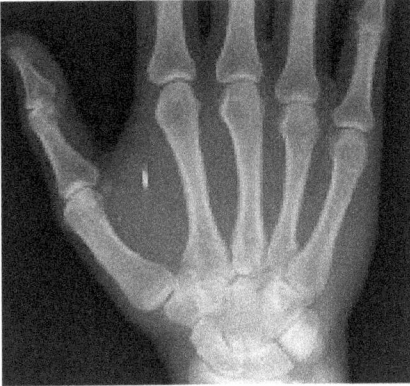

Sitting in a chair chained

My wrists and feet are tied

I'm not worried about a thing

I've already chosen a side

A man walks in

With pliers in his hand

A mask on his face

A couple tools placed on a stand

James vs. Darek

I don't want to do this he says

Please take the mark

I refuse proudly and say

I no longer live in the dark

I tell him, I like you am a solider

And God is my commander and chief

And before I finished my next sentence

He started pulling out my teeth

I know this hurts he says

Just take the mark please

I shake my head no

He took a bat to my knees

Are you ready for the mark?

I say God never fails

He took a deep breath

And one by one

He started pulling out my nails

Are you ready now! He screams

James vs. Darek

And pulls out a gun

The door opens behind him

And in walks my son...

Daddy! He cries

My eyes instantly turn red

He grabs my son by the collar

And aims the gun at his head

The mark or his life he says

You got everything to lose...

Do I? I asked myself...

What is it you would choose?

TIME

Do you believe in Jesus?

Yea he's cool

I heard about him from a few people

I've heard about him in school

Do you believe in Jesus?

I heard he died for me

I'll get to know him one day

Just need my time to be free

Do you believe in Jesus?

Yea I post prayers online

You see the one I posted

Next to the pictures of my bare behind

Do you believe in Jesus?

I praise him when I get paid

I praise him when I have a good day

I praise him when I get laid

James vs. Darek

Do you believe in Jesus?

Yea but I'll wait til I live my life

Have a few kids, settle down

After I find myself a wife

Now it's time to die

Did you believe in me?

Yes I did, I made posts online

Jesus, didn't you see?

I wanted you to believe

Jesus I'm no liar

Jesus where did you go?

And why do I smell fire??

BIGGEST FEAR

I drop a dollar in a cup

I serve dinner to the homeless on
thanksgiving

They get the same food I get

With allllll of the trimmings

I go to church on Saturday

Just like God told me

I don't sin on that day

I keep the day holy

I pray for me

I pray for you

I tell God I'll do

Whatever he asks me to

I don't steal or kill

I honor my father and mother

I love everyone the same

I treat a stranger like my brother

James vs. Darek

I see the light now

I'm standing at the gate

I'm waiting in line with a smile

Ready to seal my fate

I'm standing and planning

When I get to heaven what I'm going to do

It's my turn next; he looks at me and
says

"I never knew you"

YOU

I must say, I'm glad you're finally gone

There had to be some point, where a line was drawn

You say we have a history

But truthfully it's just based off time

We didn't go through anything; I don't
even pay you any mind

I originally wanted your friend

But it was you that called

I would've hung up on you the first day

If I knew you'd turn out to be fraud

You gave up what I wanted; to a man you
didn't even know

But made me wait forever

So I wouldn't think you were a h*??

T forgot about all that, and still made
plans

I'd leave her for you, and finally be
your man

You didn't answer my phone calls

It was definitely a top 5 heartbreak

If you died I wouldn't have cared

As far as I was concerned, you were fake

You had baby after baby after baby

James vs. Darek

And still tried to come back

I know you thought I'd take you in

It was a pleasure, turning my back

Every time I turned you down, you ran to
find another

Eventually found yourself f**king

A man I called my brother…

…fuck you

"SHE"

When we first met

I didn't like her style

I didn't like her shoes

I thought she had a funny smile

We kissed and we hugged

Then I slowly walked back home

My plan was to have sex with her

Then politely leave her alone

I had someone at the time

But we were going through a rough patch

We both had pride issues

And considered ourselves "The Catch"

So I went back to my old ways

And went back knee deep in the game

Where I played the main character

And the game was always the same

The next night "she" and me watched a movie and had sex

I wasn't too prepared for what happened next

She put hickeys on my neck

What was I supposed to do?

I was pissed at my girl

But I didn't consider us to be through

My girlfriend saw my neck the next day
She cried...and she left
I called, she didn't answer
I tried to play hard...but I wept

I was ok after a while
To the right of me was "she"
My mind was, elsewhere
But "she" was into me

I told her to leave me
But she stayed by my side
Wherever I was going
She was willing to take that ride

So I gambled on her
I dove all the way in
I did everything for her

Where do I begin?

James vs. Darek

I taught her how to drive

I bought her very first car

I listened to her expectations

And made her raise the bar

Her mom threw her out

I told her to come live with me

I did everything for her

All she had to do was love me

I made her trim her nails

To have presentable fingers

And got her haircut

Like her favorite pop singer

I worked my ass off for her

I wanted to make her complete

The first house I moved her into

Was 4,000 square feet

Our cars were the current year

And spotless I must say

James vs. Darek

Her gas tank was full

And she ate well, everyday

But after a while

My extra became the norm

She started complaining day after day

And the "Bitch" was born

The romance was fading

And the fun dwindled down

I started to feel uncomfortable

Whenever she was around

Many wanted to take her place

And in came the offers

But they could end up the same as "she"

So I didn't even bother

When things got worse

My itch came back

When you stress a crack head out hard
enough

James vs. Darek

He eventually leaves, to go find crack

I didn't want to relapse

I only needed a taste

So the strip club, as some of you know

Became my favorite place

I entertained women

Since they were being so nice

They were the opposite of "she"

So talking to them would for the moment
suffice

I was to the point where I wanted her to
leave me alone

I went to play ball one day

...and left my unlocked phone

I could've turned around

Went back home and grabbed it

I thought about it and said

"Fuck it, is she wants it she can have
it"

James vs. Darek

When I came back home

She tried to physically attack me

She punched me in the chest

And attempted to reach over and smack me

She went through my text messages

And called 3 to 5 girls

None really said anything

But one devastated her world

I stuck my chest out

And willingly admitted my guilt

And said "she" was the blame

Truthfully I didn't give a fuck how she felt

She yelled and her tears just flowed like a fountain

I'm thinking

"B*tch...sit yo a*s down this house cost me 632 thousand"

She turned into something I never wanted to see

She developed a part of her

That was just as evil as me

We both did our dirt

We've been through the absolute worst

Some days I can't tell if were each
other's gift

Or were we each other's curse

Should I leave?

Should I stay?

Yes, no, maybe?

She answered those questions for me

By getting pregnant

...and having my baby

...TO BE CONTINUED

THANK YOU

I would like to take the time out to
thank the following people for their
support.

- Jesus Christ

- Dillan Green

- Willie Green

- Joyce Green

- Wendy Peterson

- Ashley Riley

- Jade Ashton

- Crystal Hunter

- Calina Black

- Jonnetta Macon

- Heaven Peterson

- Donte Robinson

- Luchia Ramey

- Ivy Lee

- Dorlea Peoples

- Quionna Griffin

James vs. Darek

AVAILABLE AT
WWW.DDAPUBLISHING.COM

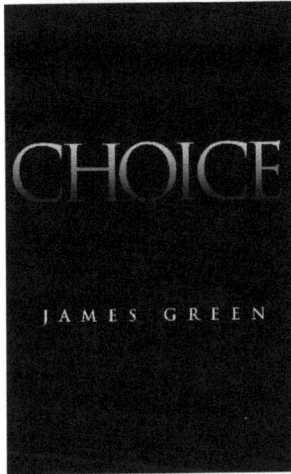

CHOICE

JAMES GREEN

This is the story of Christian L. Smith. He becomes obsessed with searching for the truth about God, the Devil...and about life itself. When in quest for that magnitude of truth, eventually you are forced to make a choice.

This is a story of love, hate, jealousy, murder and deception. Christian Smith finds himself on a journey that there's no turning back on...it will be one he will never forget.

JAMES VS DAREK II

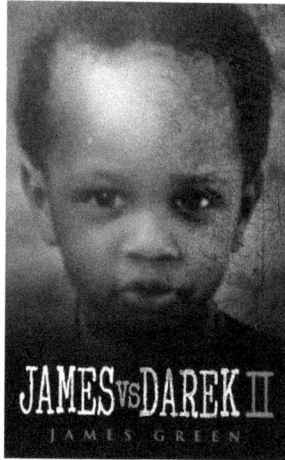

As time goes by, life goes on. Life may not turn out how we want it to or how we expect it but what is inevitable, it does goes on. Since my last entry I've been faced with more of life's turmoil, more temptation, more challenges. My relationships with my loved ones have changed, my relationship with God has been tested. So once again here are my thoughts poured out on these few sheets of paper...

www.ingramcontent.com/pod-product-compliance
Lightning Source LLC
Chambersburg PA
CBHW061149040426
42445CB00013B/1622